HOW TO SET-UP YOUR BUSINESS FOR UNDER $1000

By Dan Fleyshman
& Branden Hampton

ISBN 978-0-9974203-1-9

WWW.BUYTHISBOOK.COM

EMAIL: CONTACT@BUYTHISBOOK.COM

GIVE FEEDBACK ON THE BOOK AT:
FEEDBACK@BUYTHISBOOK.COM

PRINTED IN U.S.A

COVER BY: MOISES AGUILAR

Whenever someone asks me to give them
my best business advice, I always say...

"don't talk about it, be about it."

I've come across countless people who constantly
brag about their next great business idea, but
most never act on it.

In today's world, the media glamorizes startups able to
raise tons of money in seed funding from investors. While
this has helped inspire more people to launch businesses, I
believe it has also fueled the notion that tons of funding is
needed in order to actually start.

Well folks...
I'm here to tell youthat this is simply NOT TRUE.

This flawed belief is the exact reason why Branden
Hampton and I wrote this book.

DAN FLEYSHMAN

I started in the business world at the tender age of four. My parents owned three Levi's stores back then and I'd help them sell jeans on the weekend at a local swap meet.

I set up shop next to their booth to buy, sell, and trade baseball cards.

In high school, I worked three jobs: working at Ruby's diner as a host, at Qualcomm stadium selling snacks and worked for a stock broker simultaneously.

I became the youngest founder of a publicly traded company in history. At the age of 23, after selling 15 million dollars worth of clothing in six department store chains and surpassing expectations with our 9.5 million dollar licensing deal with STARTER apparel, we launched the "Who's Your Daddy" energy drink into 55,000 retail stores and military bases. 10 years after starting our licensing company in high school, I went on to launch Victory Poker in 2010, building the third largest team of professional players out of the 550 poker sites on the market.

Then I became a very active Angel Investor and advisor to 24+ companies that range from mobile apps & tech companies, to successful monthly box subscription sites like "DollarBeardClub" and consumer products like Uwheels, both of which exceeded $5,000,000 in sales in less than 8 months.

During all of this, I supported 2 dozen diverse charities before finally launching my own: www.modelcitizenfund. org creates backpacks filled with over 150 emergency supply items for the homeless. It has been the official charity of the World Series of Poker Europe and featured on Fox Sports, NBC, MTV, and ESPN for supplying homeless shelters, teen abuse shelters, and orphanages around the world.

Besides my passion for philanthropy, I'm also an avid poker player with multiple 1st place wins. These range from the 5k C.E.O. Poker Championship at the Palms, the Canadian Poker Tour Main Event, and the 25k high roller event at the Commerce Casino — as well as winning the 10k Chipleader Challenge at the Hard Rock.

On top of all of this, "Elevator Nights" is the quarterly event that we hold (free of charge) for 12 companies to present for five minutes each to 150 of our angel investor friends.

Currently our media site, 1stSlice.com, has generated 300,000,000 page views in the first nine months since launching — and is on pace to surpass one billion page views in 2016!

BRANDEN HAMPTON

I've spent the last half of my life building brands and becoming a master marketer. I have conquered algorithms and created dozens of methods on hacking success with social media. I was one of the first social media influencers in the world, so early that "social media influencer" wasn't even a thing yet.

I was previously rated by Forbes the #1 social media influencer in the world, I've spent the past 6 years on social media and have amassed a network of over 32,000,000 followers. My main focus is obtaining and growing some of the most premium handles in the highest monetizing spaces like @fitness, @marijuana, @makeup, @beauty, @weddings, and dozens of others.

The past few years, Dan and I have taken a Shark-Tank-Like approach to investing our time, energy and resources into growing businesses and are rewarded by taking a vested interest in those companies. We currently have a portfolio of nearly 3 dozen companies that we help with every aspect of their business.

WHY YOU SHOULD READ THIS BOOK

Since Branden and I became partners three years ago, we've invested in and co-founded 24 companies together. Most recently, we founded 1stSlice.com, a budding viral media startup that has garnered over 300 million pageviews within the first eight months of launch. The site has also received digital endorsements by influencers like Justin Bieber and Floyd Mayweather.

We've worked with some of the best entrepreneurs in the world and have started successful companies from a multitude of industries ranging from software to hardware, physical products to digital apps. You name it, we've done it.

While this book isn't necessarily a shortcut to success, it's a shortcut to finding out the best and most optimal tools to launch your early-stage startup -- without depending on major capital. These are tools that we've discovered through years of hard work and trial and error. The good news for you is that we're saving you from all the grunt work and compiling everything we've learned into one book

HOW TO READ THIS BOOK

We've structured this book where we walk you through building and growing your business from start to finish. At the end, we provide a list of resources to help you with execution.

Our hope is that this book will save you time and money, so you can focus on what's truly important in getting your company to the next level. So without further adieu, let's get started!

TABLE OF CONTENTS

CHAPTER 1:
CHECKLIST

DAN FLEYSHMAN & BRANDEN HAMPTION

THE CHECKLIST

1. Have a great idea! ☐

2. Come up with a memorable, easy to spell, catchy business name. ☐

3. Research the overall industry, competitors and every detail you can find. ☐

4. Figure out how much it's going to cost to start & operate your business. ☐

5. Ask your family, friends and associates what they think about your business. ☐

6. Determine how you will finance each stage of the business. ☐

7. Write the Executive Summary. ☐

8. Write the business plan. ☐

9. Register your website domain name. ☐

10. Register the name spelled exactly the same across all major social media platforms. ☐

11. Fill out the same bio on Facebook, Instagram, Twitter, Pinterest, Snapchat, Youtube. ☐

12. File for a corporation, partnership, LLC, once you've determined legal structure. ☐

13. Do your SWOT Analysis. ☐

14. Register a Business Name ("Doing Business As") with your state government. ☐

15. Get a Tax Identification Number. ☐

THE CHECKLIST

16. Register for State and Local Taxes. ☐

17. Open a bank account. ☐

18. Obtain business licenses and permits.
(Federal, state and local when applicable.) ☐

19. Search and apply for trademark, patent
on USPTO.gov when applicable. ☐

20. Build a website. ☐

21. Make logo, business cards, letterhead, invoice,
purchase order forms, sales sheet. ☐

22. Set-up a payment processor to handle your transactions. ☐

23. Create an accounting system. ☐

24. Search for conventions, trade shows, networking
events to attend. ☐

25. Find business vendors, suppliers, service providers
potential partners. ☐

26. Look for a business mentor that can help guide you. ☐

27. Refine your pitch ☐

28. Prepare your marketing plan. ☐

29. Scream from the mountaintops about your company
to get people to support you. ☐

30. SELL, SELL, SELL!!! ☐

20 QUESTIONS
BEFORE STARTING

Ask yourself these 20 questions to make sure you're thinking about the right key business decisions:

Why am I starting a business?

What kind of business do I want?

Who is my ideal customer?

What products or services will my business provide?

Am I prepared to spend the time and money needed to get my business started?

What differentiates my business idea and the products or services I will provide from others in the market?

Where will my business be located?

How many employees will I need?

What types of suppliers do I need?

How much money do I need to get started?

Will I need to get a loan?

How soon will it take before my products or services are available?

How long do I have until I start making a profit?

Who is my competition?

How will I price my product compared to my competition?

How will I set up the legal structure of my business?

What taxes do I need to pay?

What kind of insurance do I need?

How will I manage my business?

How will I advertise my business?

CHAPTER 2:
SETTING UP SHOP

DAN FLEYSHMAN & BRANDEN HAMPTION

SETTING UP SHOP

There are a number of things you need to do in order to ensure you have a solid and painless launch. The majority of them are inexpensive or free. Building a solid foundation of your company will help make sure you avoid drastic problems in the future.

SET UP A BUSINESS PLAN

If you're looking for funding for a new or existing business, you need a business plan. Your business plan gives lenders and investors the information they need to determine whether or not they should consider your company. A business plan is an essential roadmap for business success. This living document generally projects 3-5 years ahead and outlines the route a company intends to take to grow revenues.

Keep your business plan 20 pages or less when you're not raising Venture Capital money. This is a great exercise for you when thinking about plans for your company. You may even discover things about your company that you wouldn't have before if you didn't do it. Lastly, plan out your financials with someone who understands basic accounting.

FORMING YOUR COMPANY

Choosing and registering your business name is a key step to legally operating your business and potentially obtaining financial aid from the government. Here are the steps you need to take to all all your bases covered.

Choosing and registering your business name is a key step to legally operating your business and potentially obtaining financial aid from the government. Here are the steps you need to take to all all your bases covered.

- **Register Your Business Name**
  After you have selected a name for your business, you will need to register it to comply with the law.

- **Register With State Agencies**
  For some businesses, you need to register your business name with state or local government agency. Make sure to find out what the requirements are for your state.

SBA.gov has a TON of pertinent information for you and links + good explanations of what & how to do things for your business.

BUSINESS LICENSES & PERMITS

To run your business legally, there are certain federal and state licenses and permits you will need to obtain. These resources will help you understand the requirements for your small business

- Federal Licenses & Permits

Certain businesses, like ones that sell alcohol or firearms, require a federal license or permit. Find out which ones impact your business and how you can comply.

- State Licenses & Permits

Some states have requirements for specific businesses. Find out what business licenses and permits you need in your state.

CHOOSE YOUR BUSINESS STRUCTURE

The business structure you choose will have legal and tax implications. Learn about the different types of business structures and find the one best suited for your business.

Sole Proprietorship

A sole proprietorship is the most basic type of business to establish. You alone own the company and are responsible for its assets and liabilities. Learn more about the sole proprietor structure.

Limited Liability Company

An LLC is designed to provide the limited liability features of a corporation and the tax efficiencies and operational flexibility of a partnership. Learn more about how LLCs are structured.

Cooperative

People form cooperatives to meet a collective need or to provide a service that benefits all member-owners. Learn more about how cooperatives are structured.

Corporation

A corporation is more complex and generally suggested for larger, established companies with multiple employees. Learn more about how Corporations are structured.

Partnership

There are several different types of partnerships, which

depend on the nature of the arrangement and partner responsibility for the business. Learn more about how these are structured.

S Corporation

An S corporation is similar to a C corporation but you are taxed only on the personal level. Learn more about how S corporations are structured.

AFTER YOU'VE FORMED YOUR COMPANY

Get an EIN at the IRS website

This one is specific to the USA, but all companies need an Employer Identification Number (EIN). You can apply for one online at the irs.gov in about 5 minutes by clicking here. List yourself as a sole proprietor for now.

Setup Your Business Financials

Get a free business checking account. This will allow you to keep your business's money separate and track it (vitally important!). I like free business checking. They will also give you a debit card to track your expenses (never use a credit card) which are currently zero! Then get a Paypal account and link it to your business account so you can accept payments.

Choose a domain name

The fastest ways to get eyeballs on your new business is the internet these days. Choose a domain name that is a keyword phrase your potential customers might type into a search engine. So if you are offering salsa lessons in Bos ton, you might choose "SalsaLessonsBoston.com". The benefit of doing this is that you will most likely end up on the first page of Google results for that keyword phrase within a month or two. This will bring your customers, and is much better than showing up on the first page for "John Smith's Salsa Company" or something that no one ever searches for.

Make a simple website

The fastest way I know of to launch a website is using WordPress (wordpress.com or wordpress.org). If you don't mind using a subdomain like "mydomain.wordpress. com" it's free. But even if you want your own domain you can get one with WordPress pre-installed for about $70/year. WordPress comes with over 2500 "themes" to change the look and a great back end interface to edit the pages just like you're in Microsoft word. LifeHack. org uses Wordpress as do many other popular sites.

Set Your Prices

Most first time entrepreneurs set their prices too low. People assume low prices mean low quality, and you are worth more. Give away your product or service to the first five customers free if you'd like (it will help built buzz and you can ask them for testimonials), but after that set your price in the top 1/3 of your industry. It's always easier to lower them than to raise them.

Hiring Without Breaking the Bank

One of the biggest things that determine a company's success is the team behind it. However, not all companies have the luxury of endless capital to hire the best and brightest.

So you'll need to get creative! Here are the best and most optimal ways to find the best people to execute your vision.

Hire freelancers: Sites like upwork.com can help you find quality freelancers overseas where the cost of living is low and avoid long-term commitments. This is very useful when you're an early-stage company and can't afford full-time salaried employees.

Hire Interns: Interns are typically free and eager and of-tentimes, it's mandatory that they work a certain amount of hours to graduate from trade schools. It's also great on their resume because they're learning real world experience from your successes and failures while helping you for FREE.

Partner with other companies: When you're running on limited resources, somtimes you'll need to get creative if you want to get things done. One of these ways is to find other companies to partner with. For example, if you sell video production equipment, you can find a company that makes video content, and offer to let them use your equipment in exchange for them to promote your brand. Focus on the things you have the other people need and vice versa.

Form an advisory board

When applicable, you can ask 3 to 5 successful business people to join your advisory board in exchange for a small percentage of equity for their time and advice.

This can be very beneficial in all stages of your company since sometimes these successful business advisors lend their relationships along with their tips that can save you money, time and energy since they've already been thru so many aspects of the business life cycle.

There's many different structures from 0 to 1% on average per advisor but for example we usually give 1% which is on the high side because we want our high net worth advisors to feel invested into our deals, and care.

Some people like to give 0.25% or .05% vesting over 2 years but we only ask advisors that we trust to be apart of our company and give them the whole 1% up front and trusting that they will perform.

So adjust accordingly based on your relationships, if they're strangers (meaning a referral from a friend that's willing to do it but you have no previous business/social experience with them.) then you should probably offer closer to 0.25% per year for their help if you want to have an advisory board.

We don't do this for all of our companies, but we definitely like to have advisory board members on some of them that we can utilize their help on.

Open a bank account

As mentioned above, once you have your corporate paperwork approved, you'll want and need to open a bank account. Ideally a bank that's nearby your office or home. Make sure only the absolute most necessary people have authority access on the account.

Order check cards and a checkbook, but be wary of business credit cards until you have financing or sales, you don't want to rack up a credit card debt to fund your business.

Keeping good records is critical. Set up online banking so you can see everything at anytime.

CHAPTER 3: BUSINESS PLAN

TEMPLATE FOR BUSINESS PLAN

In the business plan outline below, you will see the ten (10) sections common to business plans, and the twenty-three (23) sub-sections you must complete.

Section I – Executive Summary

The Executive Summary is the most important part of your business plan. Because if it doesn't interest readers, they'll never even get to the rest of your plan.

Start your Executive Summary with a brief and concise explanation of what your company does. Next, explain why your company is uniquely qualified to succeed. For example, does your management team have unique competencies? Do you have any patents? Are you the first mover in your market? Does a huge, unmet market opportunity exist? Etc.

Finally, include a synopsis of your financial projections in your Executive Summary. Specifically, include your expected revenues, expenses and profits for each of the next five years, how much funding you are seeking, and the key uses of these funds.

Section II – Company Overview

The Company Overview section provides a brief history of your company.

Here you will answer questions such as when and how your organization was formed, what type of legal entity you are, and accomplishments to date.

Importantly, your past accomplishments are perhaps the best indicator of potential future success, so be sure to identify and include all key milestones your company has achieved to date. If you're brand new, then personal past accomplishments of your top execs previous companies will help show that this isn't your first rodeo. (If it is your first company, then bring on advisors or consultant's that have had successful companies in a similar space to help guide you!)

Section III – Industry Analysis

Your Industry Analysis section has two sub-sections as follows:

The Market Overview section discusses the size and characteristics of your market. For example, if you are a restaurant, you would include the size of the restaurant market, a brief discussion of sectors (e.g., fast food versus fine dining) and market trends.

5 - Relevant Market Size

The relevant market size is a much more specific calculation of your market size. It is the annual revenue your company could attain if it attained 100% market share. Your relevant market size is calculated by multiplying 1) the number of customers who might be interested in purchasing your products and/or services each year and 2) the amount these customers might be willing to spend, on an annual basis, on your products and/or services.

Section IV – Customer Analysis

Your Customer Analysis section has two sub-sections as follows:

Your Target Customers section precisely identifies your current and/or intended customers. Include as much demographic data on your target customers as possible, such as their gender, age, salary, geography, marital status and education.

6 – Customer Needs

In this section of your business plan, specify why customers want or need your products and/or services. For example, do customers care most about speed, quality, location, reliability, comfort, price, value, etc.?

Section V – Competitive Analysis

Your Competitive Analysis section has three sub-sections as follows:

7 – Direct Competitors

Direct competitors are companies that fill the same customer need you fill with the same solution. For example, if you operate an Italian restaurant, other Italian restaurants would be direct competitors.

In this section of your business plan, outline who your direct competitors are, and their strengths and weaknesses.

8 – Indirect Competitors

Indirect competitors are companies that fill the same customer need you fill with a different solution. For example, if you operate an Italian restaurant, a French restaurant would be an indirect competitor.

In this section of your business plan, outline who your indirect competitors are, and their strengths and weaknesses.

9 – Competitive Advantages

Importantly, identify your Competitive Advantages in this section. Specifically, state what is it about your company that will allow you to effectively compete (and win) against both direct and indirect competitors.

Section VI – Marketing Plan

Your Marketing Plan section has four sub-sections as follows:

10 – Products & Services

Here is where you give the details of the products and/or services your company offers.

11 – Pricing

Detail your pricing here. In particular, discuss how your pricing relates to competition. For example, are you the premium brand? The low cost brand?

Discuss your expected branding based on your chosen pricing model.

12 – Promotions Plan

Your promotions plan details the tactics you will use to attract new customers. For example, you might choose social medai advertising, or online pay-per-click ads, or press releases, and so on. In this section, detail each form of promotions you will use.

13 – Distribution Plan

Your Distribution Plan outlines the ways in which customers can buy from you. In many cases, they can only buy directly from you, perhaps at your physical location or website. In other cases, you might have distributors or partners who sell your products or services. In such a case, detail this structure.

Section VII – Operations Plan

Your Operations Plan section has two sub-sections as follows:

14 – Key Operational Processes

Your Key Operational Processes are the daily functions your business must conduct. In this section, you will detail these functions. For example, will you maintain a Customer Service department? If so, what specific role will it fill?

By completing this section, you'll get great clarity on the organization you hope to build.

15 – Milestones

In this section of your business plan, list the key milestones you hope to achieve in the future and the target dates for achieving them.

Here is where you set goals for specific and critical undertakings, such as when a new product will be created and launched, by when you plan to execute new partnerships, etc.

Section VIII – Management Team

Your Management Team section has three sub-sections as follows:

16 – Management Team Members

This section details the current members of your management team and their backgrounds.

17 – Management Team Gaps

Particularly if you're a startup venture, you will have holes in your team; roles that you'd like to fill later. Identify such roles here, and the qualifications of the people you will seek later to fill them.

18 – Board Members

If you maintain a Board of Advisors or Board of Directors, detail your Board members and their bios in this section.

Section IX – Financial Plan

Your Financial Plan section has four sub-sections as follows:

19 – Revenue Model

As simple as it seems, this section of your business plan gives clarity on how you generate revenues. Do you sell products? Do you sell advertising space? Do you sell by-products, like data? Do you sell all of the above?

20 - Financial Highlights

Your full financial model (income statement, balance sheet and cash flow statement) belong in your Appendix, but in this section you'll include the highlights.

For instance, include your revenues, key expenses, and projected net income for the next three years.

21 – Funding Requirements/Use of Funds

If you are seeking funding for your company, detail the amount here, and importantly for what you will use the funds.

22 – Exit Strategy

Particularly if you are seeking equity funding, detail your expected exit strategy. The most likely exit strategy is to sell your company to a larger firm. If so, detail the types of firms that might be interested in purchasing you and why. List the specific names of potential acquirers if applicable.

Section X – Appendix

23 – Supporting Documentation

As mentioned above, your full financial model (income statement, balance sheet and cash flow statement) belong in your appendix. Likewise, include any supporting documentation that will help convince readers your company will succeed. For example, include customer lists, awards, and patents received among others.

CHAPTER 4: EXECUTIVE SUMMARY

EXECUTIVE SUMMARY

The executive summary is often considered the most important section of a business plan. This section briefly tells your reader where your company is, where you want to take it, and why your business idea will be successful. If you are seeking financing, the executive summary is also your first opportunity to grab a potential investor's interest.

Although it's great learning experience to write a full fledged business plan like the one described in the previous chapter, for the most part, you can focus on creating an Executive Summary first to research, learn, understand and be able to present your business to someone quickly & effectively.

The Executive Summary is much more practical and useful for the early stage's of setting up your company, however I wanted to give the full overview above so that you could be prepared for when the time comes that you need the complete business plan.

1. Who/what/when/where/why/how
2. Customer problem
3. Your solution
4. Business model (how you make money)
5. Target market (who is your customer and how many of them are there)
6. Competitive advantage
7. Management team
8. Financial summary
9. Funding required

WHAT TO INCLUDE

Below are several key points that your executive summary should include based on the stage of your business.

If You Are an Established Business

If you are an established business, be sure to include the following information:

- The Mission Statement – This explains what your business is all about. It should be between several sentences and a paragraph.

- Company Information – Include a short statement that covers when your business was formed, the names of the founders and their roles, your number of employees, and your business location(s).

- Growth Highlights – Include examples of company growth, such as financial or market highlights (for example, "XYZ Firm increased profit margins and market share year-over-year since its foundation). Graphs and charts can be helpful in this section.

- Your Products/Services -- Briefly describe the products or services you provide.

- Financial Information – If you are seeking financing, include any information about your current bank and investors.

- Summarize future plans – Explain where you would like to take your business.

With the exception of the mission statement, all of the information in the executive summary should be covered in a concise fashion and kept to one page. The executive summary is the first part of your business plan many people will see, so each word should count.

IF YOU ARE A STARTUP OR NEW BUSINESS

If you are just starting a business, you won't have as much information as an established company. Instead, focus on your experience and background as well as the decisions that led you to start this particular enterprise.

Demonstrate that you have done thorough market analysis. Include information about a need or gap in your target market, and how your particular solutions can fill it. Convince the reader that you can succeed in your target market, then address your future plans.

Other than business plans, executive summaries are probably the most crucial of all business documents. It's fair to say that almost every big decision inside any company of any size involved an executive summary during the decision-making process.

Unfortunately, many people wrongly believe that an executive summary is a summary of the document, like a "Cliff Notes."

The purpose of an executive summary is to recommend a decision.

Here's how to write an executive summary that will convince an executive (or executive team) to make a decision:

1. Describe a problem, need or goal.

Underneath the words "EXECUTIVE SUMMARY" explain in one or two sentences (at most) why a decision is needed. Be specific and include quantifiable measurements, if possible.

Wrong:

This document describes the XYZ solution in detail. Here is a summary of its contents...

Right:

We are experiencing a $10 million shortfall in yearly revenue due to telecommunications network outages.

2. Describe the desired outcome.

In one or two sentences (at most) describe what will be different if the problem is solved, the need is fulfilled, or the goal is achieved. Do not provide any details of the solution.

Wrong:

In Chapter 1, we describe the multiple standard-compliant analog flux capacitors...

Right:

According to our estimates (see Section 1), reducing or eliminating these outages will increase our profitability by as much as 20%.

3. Describe your proposed solution.

Under the word "PROPOSAL," describe in a series of short paragraphs the element of your solution to the problem (as in Step 1) which will create the desired outcome (as in Step 2).

In each paragraph, refer to the sections in the larger document where that part of your solution is described in detail. Make each paragraph crisp and readable. Avoid jargon, biz-blab and needless abstractions. If at all possible, arrange the paragraphs into a step-by-step plan.

Wrong:

Leveraging our existing infrastructure will capitalize past technology investments while optimizing retraining requirements. The enhanced reliability will cause our mission-critical productivity to explode, thereby creating a monetized competitive edge.

Right:

To address the above problem, we propose the following:

Purchase and install a pilot system. This will allow us to test the new software without endangering our day-to-day operations. The requirements for this pilot system are described in Section 4.

4. Explain how you'll overcome risks.

Every business decision that's not a no-brainer involves some level of risk. Therefore, under the heading "RISKS" briefly describe those risks and how you propose to overcome them (or why they're not really a risk).

Once again, keep these paragraphs tight. Use plain language. As with the previous step, tie each paragraph to the relevant section of the longer document.

Wrong:

The proposed solution is vendor agnostic and integrates into multiple system architectures through the use of customized execute-ready scripts...

Right:

To convert the entire customer service department, we'll need to retrain our service personnel, which could reduce the department's response time. However, we plan to reduce that possibility by writing a customized training manual.

5. Ask for the decision you want made.

Under the heading "RECOMMENDATION" describe in as few words as possible, the decision that you'd like the executive(s) to make. Be specific.

If the decision involves money include the amount. If there are reasons that the decision must be made by a certain time, surface them.

Wrong:

Our ongoing concern about phone system outages continues to impact our company and therefore should be addressed in an expeditious manner.

Right:

To complete this project by the end of the current fiscal year without disrupting our current operations, we need you to approve an increase of $2 million in next quarter's IT budget.

SAMPLE EXECUTIVE SUMMARIES

Below are the two executive summaries described above as they'd actually appear. Lest you think that the first example is artificially opaque, I assure you that I personally have seen worse. Far worse.

Wrong:

EXECUTIVE SUMMARY

This document describes the XYZ solution in detail. Here is a summary of its contents:

In Chapter 1, we describe the multiple standard-compliant analog flux capacitors...

Leveraging our existing infrastructure will capitalize past technology investments while optimizing retraining requirements. The enhanced reliability will cause our mission-critical productivity to explode, thereby creating a monetized competitive edge. The proposed solution is vendor agnostic and integrates into multiple system architectures through the use of customized execute-ready scripts.

Our ongoing concern about phone system outages continues to impact our company and therefore should be addressed in an expeditious manner.

Right:

EXECUTIVE SUMMARY
We are experiencing a $10 million shortfall in yearly revenue due to telecommunications network outages.

According to our estimates (see Section 1), reducing or eliminating these outages will increase our profitability by as much as 20%.

PROPOSAL

To address the above problem, we propose the following:

Purchase and install a pilot system. This will allow us to test the new software without endangering our day-to-day operations. The requirements for this pilot system are described in Section 4.

RISKS

Possibility of lower response time. In Stage 3 of the above plan, we'll need to retrain our service personnel, which could temporarily reduce the department's average response time. However, we plan to reduce that possibility by writing a customized training manual.

RECOMMENDATION

To complete this project by the end of the current fiscal year without disrupting our current operations, we need you to approve an increase of $2 million in next quarter's IT budget.

Seriously, which of those two executive summaries do YOU think is likely to lead to the best decision?

CHAPTER 5:
S.W.O.T. ANALYSIS

S.W.O.T. ANALYSIS

When examining the potential for a new business or product, a SWOT analysis can help determine the likely risks and rewards. SWOT, which stands for Strengths, Weaknesses, Opportunities and Threats, is an analytical framework that can help your company face its greatest challenges and find its most promising new markets.

SWOT analysis was created in the 1960s by business gurus Edmund P. Learned, C. Roland Christensen, Kenneth Andrews and William D. Book. While the tool was originally intended for business use, it has since been adopted to aid personal development.

SWOT analysis gives businesses a unique way of re-evaluating their positions. The ideal outcome of a SWOT is accurate data that can be utilized to create a solid action plan for addressing a weakness and threats, and highlighting or positively exploiting your strengths and opportunities.

This analysis leads to business awareness and is the cornerstone of any successful strategic plan. It is impossible to accurately map out a small business's future without first evaluating it from all angles, which includes an exhaustive look at all internal and external resources and threats. A SWOT accomplishes this in four straight-forward steps that even rookie business owners can understand and embrace.

Many small business owners don't know how to properly use a SWOT analysis to guide their businesses.

It is about leveraging your strengths, outsourcing and partnering where you are weak, focusing on opportunities, and being aware of threats.

THE PURPOSE OF A SWOT ANALYSIS

In a business context, the SWOT analysis enables organizations to identify both internal and external influences. Outside of business, other organizations have found much use in the method's guiding principles. Community health and development, education, and other groups have used the analysis. SWOT's primary objective is to help organizations develop a full awareness of all the factors, positive and negative, that may affect strategic planning and decision making. This goal can be applied to almost any aspect of industry.

Though SWOT is meant to act primarily as an assessment technique, its lengthy record of success makes it an invaluable tool in project management.

A good SWOT analysis serves as a dashboard to your product or services, and when done correctly, can help you to navigate and implement a sound strategy for your business regardless of company size or sector. We continue to revisit ours every year to keep it updated due to constant shifts in market trends. It's a crisp and simple way to communicate the most important aspects of our brand.

When to use SWOT

SWOT is meant to be used during the proposal stage of strategic planning. It acts as a precursor to any sort of company action, which makes it appropriate for the following moments:

- Exploring avenues for new initiatives
- Making decisions about execution strategies for a new policy
- Identifying possible areas for change in a program
- Refining and redirecting efforts mid plan

The SWOT analysis is an excellent tool for organizing information, presenting solutions, identifying roadblocks and emphasizing opportunities.

Performing a SWOT analysis is a great way to improve business operations and decision-making. It allowed us to identify the key areas where our organization was performing at a high level, as well as areas that needed work. Some small business owners make the mistake of thinking about these sorts of things informally, but by taking the time to put together a formalized SWOT analysis, you can come up with ways to better capitalize on your company's strengths and improve or eliminate weaknesses.

While the business owner should certainly be involved in creating a SWOT analysis, it could be much more helpful to include other team members in the process.

Some management teams do a SWOT analysis quarterly. The collective knowledge removes blind spots that, if left undiscovered, could be detrimental to your business or your relationship with clients.

Collaborative SWOT analyses also give employees a greater sense of understanding and involvement in the company.

Businesses should not consider the SWOT analysis a cure-all however. Like any self-analysis tool, it can be used incorrectly if we allow our ego or insecurities to drive the content. It is imperative to be as honest with yourself [as possible] and be prepared to provide input that truly reflects your competencies, accomplishments and abilities.

The elements of a SWOT analysis

A SWOT analysis focuses entirely on the four elements included in the acronym, allowing companies to identify the forces influencing a strategy, action or initiative. Knowing these positive and negative elements can help companies more effectively communicate what parts of a plan need to be recognized.

When drafting a SWOT analysis, individuals typically create a table split up into four columns to list each impacting element side-by-side for comparison. Strengths and weaknesses won't typically match listed opportunities and threats, though they should correlate somewhat since they're tied together in some way.

Pairing external threats with internal weaknesses can highlight the most serious issues faced by a company.

Once you've identified your risks, you can then decide whether it is most appropriate to eliminate the internal weakness by assigning company resources to fix the problems, or reduce the external threat by abandoning the threatened area of business and meeting it after strengthening your business.

Internal factors

The first two letters in the acronym, S (Strengths) and W (Weaknesses), refer to internal factors, which means the resources and experience readily available to you. Examples of areas typically considered include:

- Financial resources, such as funding, sources of income and investment opportunities
- Physical resources, such as your company's location, facilities and equipment
- Human resources, such as employees, volunteers and target audiences
- Access to natural resources, trademarks, patents and copyrights
- Current processes, such as employee programs, department hierarchies and software systems

Businesses should also consider "softer" elements such as company culture and image, operational efficiency and potential, and the role of key staff.

When listing strengths and weaknesses, individuals shouldn't try to sugarcoat or glaze over inherent weaknesses or strengths. Identifying factors both good and bad is important in creating a thorough SWOT analysis.

Companies can't hope to take advantage of or control the external factors until the internals have been objectively assessed.

External factors

External forces influence and affect every company, organization and individual. Whether these factors are connected directly or indirectly to an opportunity or threat, it is important to take note of and document each one. External factors typically reference things you or your company do not control, such as:

- Market trends, like new products and technology or shifts in audience needs
- Economic trends, such as local, national and international financial trends
- Funding, such as donations, legislature and other sources
- Demographics, such as a target audience's age, race, gender and culture
- Relationships with suppliers and partners
- Political, environmental and economic regulations

Using SWOT to identify external factors benefited Supreme Graphics, a commercial print manufacturer, which was struggling to compete with the digital industry in retaining larger advertising and marketing clients.

SWOT ANALYSIS TEMPLATE

Here is a SWOT Analysis template with some examples filled in:

Strengths
Weaknesses

       Political support
       Funding available
       Market experience
       Strong leadership
       Project is very complex
       Likely to be costly
       May have environmental impact
       Staff resources are already stretched

Opportunities
Threats

       Project may improve local economy
       Will improve safety
       Project will boost company's public image
       Environmental constraints
       Time delays
       Opposition to change

The SWOT analysis is a simple, albeit comprehensive strategy for identifying not only the weaknesses and threats of a plan, but also the strengths and opportunities it makes possible. While an excellent brainstorming tool, the four-cornered analysis also prompts entities to examine and execute strategies in a more balanced way. However, it is not the only factor in developing a good business strategy.

A SWOT analysis is helpful in broadly addressing questions to develop a business plan, but it doesn't go far enough. The exercise alone won't identify your key value drivers of your business. Planning without first knowing your goals and the metrics by which you will measure your progress toward achieving those goals is inefficient and misguided.

A SWOT analysis is just one tool in the strategy toolbox.

When SWOT is used in conjunction with other analysis models, these frameworks for strategic thinking are well worth your time and should guide your decision making.

Additional analytic tools to consider include PEST (Political, Economic, Social and Technological), MOST (Mission, Objective, Strategies and Tactics), or SCRS (Strategy, Current state, Requirements and Solution) analyses.

Undertaking additional individual analysis in conjunction with a tool like SWOT may also help business leaders identify how they can improve their personal responses. Service-assessment tools, specifically the Mayer-Salovey-Caruso Emotional Intelligence Test (MSCEIT), which measures a respondent's abilities related to the four branches of emotional intelligence: perceiving emotions, facilitating thought, understanding emotions and managing emotions. DISC assessments are also valuable in that they provide further insight into your work styles, specifically around Dominance, Influence, Steadiness and Conscientiousness.

This information helps to determine what your motivators and triggers are, and how you handle those. By knowing these things about yourself, you can work toward an action plan of self-improvement or minimally ensure you select jobs, organizations and leaders that are an appropriate fit for you to improve your chances for success.

CHAPTER 6: GETTING YOUR FIRST CUSTOMERS

GETTING YOUR FIRST CUSTOMERS

After you've started and launched your business, finding your first customers can be a tough challenge to overcome. While big corporations and well-funded startups can afford to dump millions of dollars into ad campaigns, not everyone has such a luxury. So, most of us will need to get creative.

Go door to door, email everyone, call potential clients, hire interns, commission people to refer you sales, scream from the mountaintops, work/give discounts to the first few people just to get the initial sales going and see how the customers react to your pitch/price/paperwork/people/product.

The next five steps are all ways you can market your brand or product for the <u>price of FREE</u>.

Start Marketing on CraigsList.com

Start by making regular posts on Craigslist.com. This is a free classified website that attracts millions of viewers. You can get some traffic to your website instantly by making some posts here, and you should continue to repost them every few days.

Start a Meetup.com Group

Meetup.com helps people with similar interests get together. If a group exists in your area with potential customers, join it. Try to be invited as a guest speaker and offer value to members of the group (don't pitch them). Just by making friends and helping out you will start to bring in business. If a MeetUp group for your topic doesn't exist yet, that's even better. Start one up! You'll be viewed as the authority in the area.

Post a Video to YouTube.com

YouTube is a video sharing website, and it gets ridiculous amounts of traffic. It's actually easier to make a video than you think, and it doesn't have to be professional at all. You can record one with your digital camera, make a screen recording of your computer (even a powerpoint presentation) with software like Camtasia, or purchase a $20 webcam. Teach or show something useful, and include a link to your site at the end of the video. You will get traffic!

Network

Send an email to all your friends and family (and really everyone on your contact list) telling them about the business you just started. Put a note at the end asking them to forward the note to anyone they know who might be interested (and tell them about the free offer for the first five customers). You'll not only reach your network, but you'll reach your network's network (an exponential difference). You should also get people's business cards that you meet (far more effective than giving them since few people will write you back) and offer to help them.

Create badass content!

Even if you aren't a writer, you can put together a great article. Think of something your potential customers might want to know. Then write a "top ten" list (e.g. the top ten beginner salsa moves) or a "ten step" format (e.g. the then steps to learning salsa basics). Contact the owners of a dozen different websites that your potential customers might visit, and see if they'd like to use your article for free. Include a link to your website at the bottom in the "About the Author" section.

Make it useful.

This should go without saying, but it's often forgotten. Your content is meant to be useful for your readers and customers. By constantly asking yourself "would it be useful to them?" you will create more powerful content people want to share.

Make sharing easy.

The more easily shareable is your content, the more people will share it. This means using tools like ShareThis for content published on your blog and services like Click to Tweet that let people share your articles in seconds. Giving them rich content and media that improves the sharing experience itself, like images, quotes, or infographics, is also an important part of this optimization process.

Using this simple format, you can launch a new business in about a month, and hopefully make your first sale. But the best part is, even if it doesn't work, you've learned a priceless lesson and risked little or no money.

Don't spend a single red cent that isn't absolutely required when launching a new business! See if your idea works first, and then spend AFTER you've made your first sale!

Managing and scaling traffic to your website

Once the traffic arrives, you need to know what it's actually doing there. Are they leaving because your signup form is too complex? Or abandoning their shopping carts because of expensive shipping charges?

Google Analytics is an obvious tool every online startup must master. It's free, gives you a ton of insight and helps you figure out what is actually happening on your site.

There are a host of tools out there that help you to make better sense of people coming to your website. As KISS-metrics (a service costing between $150 and $500 per month) puts it: "Google Analytics tells you what's happening. KISSmetrics tells you who's doing it." Which is a fair statement of what it does. It gives more insight at a personal user level of the behavior of users.

Mention to monitor and react

Once people start talking about you, the best way to continue growing is to detect these mentions and to reply to every one of them. By doing so, it fosters a lot of motivation for them to talk and mention even more about you, creating a network of trusted brand advocates. By having alerts based on keywords -- like the name of your company, your products or your competitors -- mention allows you to stay in the know and react in seconds by connecting your social accounts directly to the app.

With these five tools, you'll find yourself developing and maintaining a clear brand voice in no time. And it's then that you'll start to see your online presence heating up.

Communicating with your customers on social media

When to communicate:

On average, Thursday sees the most company mentions (15.78%), followed closely by Tuesday (15.68%) and Wednesday (15.52%).

At 12.22% and 11.36% respectively, Saturday and Sunday see the fewest company mentions, presenting an opportunity that often goes unnoticed. This makes sense when you consider that most companies don't have a plan in place for social networks and other platforms over the weekend. Plan ahead and develop a content strategy for sourcing and scheduling content throughout the workweek to be posted on Saturday and Sunday.

Since Thursday is the most crowded day when it comes to brands and companies being mentioned, don't focus too much effort on a day when it's hardest to be heard above the noise.

Who to communicate with:

Only a little over 8% of your users have more than 500 followers. The other 91% of mentions may be coming from people with smaller reach, but they're far in the majority and a powerful force of 1-to-1 connections.

Simply answering a tweet in less than an hour, and not just tweets directed to you but tweets about you, can prompt people to tweet about your level of service and your product. Speed, relevancy and charm can make the difference between a product with decent word-of-mouth and an awesome viral product. Go the extra mile. Not only will the person you help appreciate the effort, so will everyone else who finds out.

Deliver the product or service fast

Your business is a work in progress and if you launch your product or service quickly, you will be able to build a community of customers who can provide valuable feedback that can help you improve the offerings. In the words of LinkedIn founder Reid Hoffman, "If you're not embarrassed by your first product release, you've released too late.

Overdeliver!

Once you land a new client/customer, be sure to go above and beyond the call of duty for at least the first few months. You'll have this customer hooked from then on and they'll be a great case study. Every customer is important, you should always try to over deliver when it doesn't hurt your companies bottom line or take up a ton of your staff's time, however it's ultra critical to nurture the first clients/customers because they will give you important feedback that will then affect how you do business with tons of future clients/customers!

Provide outstanding customer service

Interacting with people is a big part of the job. Your business may gain new customers because you made them feel important. For example, Zappos wasn't the first online store to sell shoes, but the company perfected its customer-service department and won over shoppers. They make people feel important before they buy, when they purchase, when the delivery arrives, if they call, if they complain, if they want to return the product, if they want to buy more, no matter what the scenario, Zappo's has constantly won awards on customer service and their CEO Tony Hsieh wrote a wonderful book about the subject.

Don't be overly concerned by the economy

Some of the best businesses have launched during a recession. In fact, half of the Fortune 500 companies listed in 2009 were founded during such times, according to the Ewing Marion Kauffman Foundation. So don't overprice yourself compared to the competition but don't be nervous if you've created a strong product offering at the right price.

A word of caution: Make sure clients pay their bills

Always be certain to receive payment for your products or services. Instead of being taken advantage of, establish a time frame for payment. Sounds simple, but it's extremely important for your business's survival to have your accounts receivable RECEIVED!

*A friendly reminder: Arrive at a useful definition of success

Just because your business hasn't made you a millionaire (yet) doesn't mean that your enterprise is a failure. If you're able to make some sort of profit doing something that you're passionate about, that is a success story! Set realistic goals for the type of company you're creating and I'll give you a reason to make realistic expectations for your investors, staff, loved ones.

Example: You tell your investors, staff & friends that your new online clothing store is going to surpass $1,000,000 in sales in the first year!!!

Then you only do $711,421 in sales : (so it seems like a failure that you've missed your mark by 28%

Example 2: You tell your investors, staff & friends that your new online clothing store is going to surpass $500,000 in sales in the first year!!!

Then you do $711,421 in sales :) so now you're a hero to your investors, staff, friends that you understated & over delivered to the tune of 42% higher then expectations.

Embedding Your Company into the Internet

Besides social media platforms like Instagram, Twitter, Snapchat, Facebook, Vine, Pinterest there's also review sites, forums, lists, BBB, YELP, yellowpages YP.com , LinkedIn, Wikipedia, these are all sites that you want to proactively register your business on to add credibility. It helps with organic search rankings when people search for your business online. They're free and each one only takes a few minutes to register and fill out your profile to look good.

Create a landing page: Landing pages are now a must-have design choice to boost your online special operations. By customizing these towards a targeted audience, along with specific and relatable calls to action, it makes them way more efficient at achieving higher click-through rates. Unbounce allows you to create landing pages incredibly fast, with no technical skills required, making it easy not only to build but also to A/B test and implement the best results.

Do SEO keyword research: The first step in most online businesses is getting traffic to your site in the first place. When you think about how traffic arrives at places, a common starting point is organic search traffic. SEMRush (a service that runs between $70 to $150 per month) and MOZ (one that will set you back $49 to $99 per month) are tools that both help to see how you rank for key search terms and how to better capture users. SEMrush is a SEO keyword search tool that helps to better capture organic search traffic. MOZ is not only great with SEO but also emulates Google's domain-authority ranking and gives you a sense of what competitors are doing better than you.

Prepare to get the word out: When launch day comes, startups need to get the word out to as many people to have the most impact and increase the probability of being heard in crowded industries. Often this entails getting your current followers to share with their friends, family and connections. LaunchCrew will help you do just that. It lets you cast a much wider net, practically doubling or tripling your impact. But how? By asking your audience for their credentials to be able to post on their behalf on the day of your launch. Or for any major campaign. You'll get that initial boost you've always dreamed of -- the one you really need these days to break out of the pack from the very start.

When it's time to launch your company, that week should be spent asking for every favor possible to help people get the word out. If it's a local business you don't need to ask your famous friend in another State to post about it, but every relevant favor you can ask and trade you can offer to get people excited and aware of your business. There's usually key people that are "fire starters" whom really help the initial buzz around town or around the internet.

Social media is FREE:

We could write a whole book on social media, (and we probably will.) but the most important part is for you to reserve your companies name spelled the same way across all the social platforms, with the same bio, photo, etc. so that no matter where or how someone finds your company, it's the same and easy to connect with!

You just never know if they're gonna find you on Pinterest, Facebook or Twitter, but you better look good and be ready when they do find you!!!

(There's a comprehensive list of resources at the end of this book that are mostly free & easy.)

FINAL THOUGHTS

DAN FLEYSHMAN & BRANDEN HAMPTION

FINAL THOUGHTS

After reading this book you now have a lot to think about. In addition to providing you with specific, real-world how-to advice for the different stages of starting and building a business, I've also tried to paint an accurate picture of the entrepreneur's journey. What you need to decide now is whether or not this journey is right for you.

No one is forcing you to start a company. This is not a path you must go down. Millions of people find success and happiness working for someone else. If you work for someone else you won't have to worry about finding investors, paying lawyers and accountants, securing business licenses, and all the little headaches that come with being a business owner. The entrepreneur's journey is one of the most stressful and difficult paths in business. It's not for everyone.

But here's the flip side to that. The entrepreneur's journey is also one of the most exhilarating, thrilling, and financially rewarding paths in business. It's difficult to become a millionaire working for someone else. But as an entrepreneur it's almost expected that you'll build a million dollar net worth. If one of your goals in life is to create significant wealth, entrepreneurship is perhaps the most effective route to reaching that goal.

In his book The Ten Roads to Riches, billionaire Kenneth Fisher examines all the routes to becoming wealthy, including marrying well, becoming a famous celebrity, creating patents, and working your way up to becoming the CEO of a large company. He makes it very clear that most of the ten roads are quite simply not available to or not realistic for the average person.

What are your real odds of moving to Hollywood and becoming the next George Clooney? What are the chances you'll meet, fall in love with, and marry a billionaire's son or daughter? Pretty slim. According to Fisher, the absolute best and most likely way to become rich is through founding and building your own business. I agree 100%. That's why I've chosen the entrepreneur's path.

By the way, Fisher's book stands in stark contrast to most of the other how-to-become-a-millionaire books on the market. The vast majority of how-to-become-a-millionaire books are personal finance books, not business start-up books. They preach that the way to become a millionaire is to live frugally for decades, invest wisely, buy a modest home, and after 50 years of scrimping and saving and paying off your mortgage you may reach a combined million dollar net worth. That's not bad advice, but it's a very different path. All of the entrepreneurs I know are on a mission to change the world, build value, and create wealth; they don't want to wait until they're 75 years old to be a millionaire.

But being an entrepreneur is risky. There's no getting around the age-old risk-verses-reward equation. The higher the risk, the greater the potential reward. If you're afraid to invest all your savings in a new venture, then maybe entrepreneurship isn't for you. Or maybe you just haven't found that one idea that you're totally passionate about bringing to life.

Since you're reading this book I'm going to assume you've already wrestled with the decision of whether or not to become an entrepreneur, and now you're interested in learning how. The best way to learn entrepreneurship is by doing it. Armed with the information in this book and everything else you've read, it's time to jump in.

I've met hundreds of people who say they want to start their own business. But when I ask them what steps they've taken to get started, the answer is always the same, "Umm.. uh... well... I'm still thinking about it." Just thinking about it won't get you anywhere. If you actually want to accomplish something, even if you don't think you know everything you need to know, just start. Just build the website. Build a prototype of that product that's in your head. Then take it out and show it to people. Start the process. Even if you only spend an hour a day on your idea, take those first steps.

If you can spend one hour in the morning and one hour in the evening on something, you'll be surprised at what you can accomplish in just a few months. You don't have to quit your day job or stop going to school. I'm not telling you to drop out of college, but 2 hours a day is 60 hours a month and if you put in extra hours on the weekends you can see how it adds up quickly. Work on your business as a side project until you realize it's time to actually raise some money or open up the retail location or website and start selling!

You can spend the first month, three months, or a year, depending on the kind of business, just setting aside one or two hours a day to work on it. It doesn't matter what age group you're in, when you're going to graduate, or when you're going to retire. If you start working on your idea as a side project you keep your risks low while you figure out a few important things. Is there really a market for your idea? Do you enjoy working on it? Are you willing to risk your time and money on this?

If you keep procrastinating and you can't commit to getting started, then maybe you're not an entrepreneur. But that's not necessarily a bad thing. You can still make it happen. There are millions of people who have great jobs that they love or jobs where it makes no sense to leave, like doctors, lawyers, or executives. In this case, find somebody who is an entrepreneur to do it for you. If you have a great idea for an innovative new product that nobody's ever done, but you don't want to leave your job and you don't have the free time yourself, hire someone. I guarantee you there's a college student out there, or an entrepreneur out there that will go do it for you for low pay and a piece of the company.

The important thing right now is that you stop just talking about it and actually start working on it. This idea could be your future. It could make your dreams come true. It could make you and your family wealthy. No more excuses. No more delay. Take that first step. Entrepreneurs will always find a way, so what are you waiting for? It's time to get started.

RESOURCES

IDEA GENERATION

GERM.IO
Too many awesome ideas die in lost notes and cleaned up whiteboards. germ. io lets you capture every eureka moment and helps you execute it.

EXPERIMENT BOARD
Use the lean validation/experiment board to describe, validate and refine your business idea.

CURATOR
Curator is the No.1 tool for the creative process. From the first fragment of an idea to presentation. Simple, fast, powerful.

POINT
Point is a quick way to share and discuss what you find online.

STACHE
Stache makes it quick and easy to collect pages you find useful, interesting or inspiring, in a visual and fully searchable library.

MINDMEISTER
Because of its sleek design and simple interface, MindMeister has been positioned as the number one mind mapping tool available today.

BOX NOTES
Your business ideas should live with the rest of your business content. Now they can.

SKITCH
Get your point across with fewer words using annotation, shapes and sketches, so that your ideas become reality faster.

XMIND
A more elegant way to gather, analyze and utilize knowledge, information and ideas.

ELEVATR
A fast, beautiful, and fun way to capture, organize, and share business ideas.

DOMAIN NAME RESOURCES

NAMECHEAP
Namecheap makes registering, hosting, and managing domains for yourself or others easy and affordable.

DOMAINR
Domainr helps you explore the entire domain name space beyond the ubiquitous and crowded .com, .net and .org.

NAMEBOX.IO
Buy unwanted and/or unused web domains that other people won't be using anymore.

GODADDY DOMAINFINDER

GoDaddy DomainFinder is the new domain search app that lets you build your own domain name with the world's largest domain registrar.

INSTANT DOMAIN SEARCH

Instant Domain Search is a fast and free service for finding great domain names. Find domain names instantly by searching as you type.

GO.CO

With a .CO domain, you get more than just a web address.

LEAN DOMAIN SEARCH

Lean Domain Search is a domain name generator that helps you find great available domain names for your websites.

DICTIONARY DOMAINS

Dictionary Domains offers 14,234 legit, {word}.{tld} domains that you can register and then get back to work on the important stuff.

DOMCOMP

Compare prices of over 745 top level domains from the industry's most popular registrars.

WEB HOSTING HOSTING RESOURCES

BLUEHOST

Bluehost offers the best web hosting, powering over 2 million website worldwide.

BLADEWP

BladeWP offers Clustered and Fast Wordpress hosting with 24/7 support.

RACKSPACE

Rackspace manages your cloud services. You run your business.

AMAZON WEB SERVICES

Amazon Web Services offers reliable, scalable, and inexpensive cloud computing services. Free to join, pay only for what you use.

HEROKU

Heroku provides services and tools to build, run, and scale web applications.

DIGITALOCEAN

DigitalOcean is simplifying cloud by providing an infrastructure experience that developers love.

JOYENT

High-Performance Public Cloud and Private Cloud Software Made Easy.

STATUSCAKE

Monitoring up to every 30 seconds & alerts by email, Twitter & phone.

DOTCLOUD

Assemble your stack from dozens of pre-configured components. dotCloud deploys and scales it for you.

MARKET RESEARCH

GOOGLE TRENDS
Google Trends gives you insights on search-terms, you can also compare the volume of searches between two or more terms.

VALIDATELY
Validate demand or usability on a clickable prototype or live feature with Validately.

AYTM
AYTM is a DIY survey platform with a built-in consumer panel bringing the power of consumer insights to everyone.

PROVED
Proved connects to your potential customers and benchmarks your idea against thousands of others. Fresh idea? Test. Improve. Go!

CONSUMER BAROMETER
The Consumer Barometer is a free tool that delivers consumer insights in the fast changing digital landscape.

CRUNCHBASE
CrunchBase is the world's most comprehensive dataset of startup activity and it's accessible to everyone.

SIMILARWEB
Analyze your competitors' traffic and identify growth opportunities online with SimilarWeb.

COMPASS
Compass aims to reduce the massive failure rate of businesses in a scalable way.

STATISTA
Statista is the leading international statistics portal on the internet.

HONEYBADGER
With one click, Honeybadger will show you how much traffic a site gets, how much money they raised, what powers their stack, and more.

FORMS & SURVEYS

TYPEFORM
Typeform is a free and beautiful online survey and form builder.

SURVEYPAL
Use Surveypal to design beautiful, cross-device surveys that boost response rates, start collecting responses today.

QUALAROO
Get Voice of Customer Insights that Help Your Business Grow with Qualaroo.

QUALTRICS
Qualtrics is a rapidly growing software-as-a-service company and the provider of the world's leading insight platform.

FORMSTACK
Formstack quickly lets you create and deploy the web forms you need without any coding knowledge.

DELIGHTED
Delighted uses the Net Promoter System® to gather real feedback from your customers.

PEEK
See and hear a 5-minute video of a real person using your site or app with Peek.

SURVEYMONKEY
SurveyMonkey is the simple way to create surveys: Intelligent survey software for primates of all species.

VERIFY
Verify allows you to quickly test concepts with users to get faster feedback.

GOOGLE CONSUMER SURVEYS
When you want answers to your business questions, you need to reach everyday people — Google consumer surveys helps you with that.

MOCKUPS & WIREFRAMING

MOQUPS
Moqups is the most stunning HTML5 app for creating resolution-independent SVG mockups & wireframes for your next project.

BALSAMIQ
Balsamiq Mockups is a wireframing tool to help rid the world of bad software.

MOCKINGBIRD
Mockingbird is an online tool that makes it easy for you to create, link together, preview, and share mockups of your website or application.

JUSTINMIND
Justinmind is a powerful wireframe software to define web and mobile applications.

CONCEPT.LY
Concept.ly is a Web and Mobile mockups tool. Convert wireframes and designs into interactive Apps.

RESOURCES

FLINTO
Use Flinto to create iOS and Android prototypes made from your existing screen designs.

GLIFFY
Create professional-quality flowcharts, Org charts, UML diagrams and more with Gliffy.

LUCIDCHART
Lucidchart is a flow chart maker & online diagram software.

MOCKFLOW
Design and collaborate on user interface concepts for your apps and websites with MockFlow.

OMNIGRAFFLE
OmniGraffle is for creating beautiful, precise graphics. Available for Mac and iPad.

DESIGN

UICLOUD
UICloud collects the best user interface designs from the internet and provides a search engine for you to find the best UI element you need.

UX ARCHIVE
UX Archive helps you compare the most interesting iPhone app user flows.

LITTLE BIG DETAILS
Little Big Details is a curated collection of the finer details of design, updated every day.

SKETCH
Sketch gives you the power, flexibility and speed you always wanted in a light-weight and easy-to-use package.

FEEDBAG.IO
Feedbag.io helps you collect feedback in a visual and user-friendly manner.

INVISION
Transform your Web & Mobile (iOS, Android) designs into clickable, interactive Prototypes and Mockups with InVision.

CRAYON
Crayon is the most comprehensive collection of marketing designs on the web.

PTTRNS
The finest collection of mobile design patterns, resources and inspiration.

UIGIFS
uiGIFs showcases new user interfaces in the form of animated GIFs. All of the apps showcased on the site are real, launched apps.

NAMING RESOURCES

NAMINUM
Naminum is the leading startup, company and website name generator on the web.

NAMEMESH
NameMesh helps you in finding a perfect name for your startup or business using an intelligent ranking and classification program.

NAMECHK
Check the availability of your username across dozens of the most popular social tnetwork websites with NameChk.

KNOWEM
KnowEm allows you to check for the use of your brand, product and user-name instantly on over 500 social media websites.

DOCK NAME
Dock Name is a crowdsourced service that helps startups find a domain name.

NAMEROBOT
NameRobot offers everything you need to create suitable naming ideas in a short time.

PANABEE
Panabee is a simple way to search for domain names, app and company names.

BRANDBUCKET
Explore premium, quality, hand-picked, unique and brandable business names available for sale for your business venture.

TRADEMARKIA
Trademarkia is one of the largest trademark search engines in the world. Search Millions of Trademarks Filed Since 1870 For Free.

HOW TO NAME YOUR STARTUP
The name of your startup is critically important to its success, and in this video Jason Calacanis tells you how to land an amazing name.

DEVELOPMENT

DEVDOCS
DevDocs combines multiple API documentations in a fast, organized, and searchable interface.

PUBLICAPIS
PublicAPIs is the Largest API Directory In The Galaxy.

CODEFRESH
Codefresh offers a complete development environment in the cloud, that accelerates the time required to build great cloud apps.

RESOURCES

NODE.JS
Node.js is designed to build scalable network applications.

MESSAGEBIRD
Send SMS and voice messages worldwide via MessageBird's website, email or your own software (API).

CODA
Coda is everything you need to hand-code a website, in one beautiful app.

README.IO
Crowdsource your developer hub with ReadMe.io.

STAMPLAY
Parse meets IFTTT, changing how software is built. Create advanced web and mobile apps in a fraction of the time with Stamplay.

CODEKIT
CodeKit is like steroids for web developers.

BOWERY
Bowery is the best way to set up, manage, and share your development environment.

DEPLOYMENT

GITHUB
The GitHub platform provides powerful collaboration, code review, and code management for open source and private projects.

DEPLOYDO
deploydo is a tool for deploying source code to one or multiple servers.

WERCKER
Test and deploy your applications with ease. Together, with Wercker.

DIVIDE.IO
Divide.io is an open source backend library for mobile apps.

NEW RELIC
New Relic is a software analytics company that makes sense of 250 billion data points daily from millions of applications.

CODESHIP
Release more frequently, get faster feedback and build the product your users need with Codeship.

DEPLOY
Deploy your websites or apps directly from your repository to servers or the cloud.

PAGODA BOX
Pagoda Box is an Object Oriented Hosting Framework.

ENGINE YARD
Deploy, scale and monitor your app with the Engine Yard cloud application management platform.

CIRCLECI
CircleCI is simple, powerful Continuous Integration and Deployment for developers.

SOCIAL TOOLS

DEVDOCS
DevDocs combines multiple API documentations in a fast, organized, and searchable interface.

PUBLICAPIS
PublicAPIs is the Largest API Directory In The Galaxy.

CODEFRESH
Codefresh offers a complete development environment in the cloud, that accelerates the time required to build great cloud apps.

NODE.JS
Node.js is designed to build scalable network applications.

MESSAGEBIRD
Send SMS and voice messages worldwide via MessageBird's website, email or your own software (API).

CODA
Coda is everything you need to hand-code a website, in one beautiful app.

README.IO
Crowdsource your developer hub with ReadMe.io.

STAMPLAY
Parse meets IFTTT, changing how software is built. Create advanced web and mobile apps in a fraction of the time with Stamplay.

CODEKIT
CodeKit is like steroids for web developers.

BOWERY
Bowery is the best way to set up, manage, and share your development environment.

DEPLOYMENT

BRAND24
Identify and analyze online conversations about your brand, product and competition. Easy to use, reliable and cost-effective. Brand24 is used by hundreds of businesses of all sizes.

BUFFER
Buffer is the easiest way to publish on social media.

RESOURCES

HOOTSUITE
Hootsuite is the world's most widely used social relationship platform, with more than 10 million users in 175+ countries.

TOPSY
Topsy is a social analytics company that gives you instant answers to critical business questions through real-time analysis of public conversations.

WOOBOX
Woobox helps you easily create powerful contests, sweepstakes, coupons, and more to grow your fans and amplify your marketing.

SIMPLY MEASURED
Simply Measured offers the most complete measurement solution for social media marketers.

MENTION
Media monitoring made easy with Mention. Create alerts on your name, brand, competitors and be informed in real-time of any mention on the web and social networks.

WEDGIES
Wedgies is a real-time platform that aggregates data and creates better interaction through questions.

SOCIALSENSR
SocialSensr helps organizations become people-connected companies, by offering user-friendly, state-of -the-art Social Media Management tools.

MVP

"MINIMUM VIABLE PRODUCT"

A development method to build something for the least amount of money and work in order to make a functioning product to test to see if consumers care. This can be used for online or physical products.

QUICKMVP
QuickMVP is the easiest way to test your ideas, without wasting time or money.

GENERATOR
Generator is the easiest way to make a landing page for your startup.

PROTO.IO
Proto.io is a web platform enabling users to create fully interactive mobile app prototypes.

LAUNCHROCK
Use LaunchRock to Start Now and Launch Your Landing Page in Minutes. Acquire, engage and grow your audience with powerful social sharing tools & analytics that drive user growth.

RESOURCES

INSTAPAGE
Instapage makes building and A/B split testing landing pages simple.

MARVEL
Just had the next billion-dollar app idea? Grab a pen and within minutes your idea will come to life with Marvel.

UNTORCH
Get signups with an Untorch referral campaign.

STRIKINGLY
Strikingly is an online web platform enabling individuals to build mobile-optimized websites.

BLOCS APP
Build beautiful websites without touching a line of code with Blocs app.

MARKETING

REVUE
Create an engaging, gorgeous, weekly digest. You focus on curation, Revue makes sure it looks awesome.

MAILCHIMP
More than 7 million people use MailChimp to design and send email marketing campaigns.

BRANCH METRICS
Branch Metrics helps apps grow through seamless referrals, sharing and deep linking across install.

HUBSPOT
HubSpot is the world's leading inbound marketing and sales platform with 11,500+ customers in 70+ countries.

GROWTHHACKERS
GrowthHackers is a community to learn and share about ethical online marketing techniques that drive effective, scalable and sustainable growth.

CUSTOMER.IO
Customer.io helps you send targeted human messages to your users, by utilizing their unique interactions with your business.

EXIT MONITOR
Exit Monitor converts your exiting web visitors into leads.

REALLY GOOD EMAILS
Really Good Emails is a large collection of good product email design.

PETITHACKS
petithacks showcases a collection of Acquisition, Retention, & Revenue hacks used by companies.

GLEAM
Gleam helps thousands of businesses run amazing competitions across social networks.

EARLY USERS

BETALIST
BetaList has previously covered startups such as Pinterest, IFTTT and Mailbox before they launched and made it big.

PRODUCT HUNT
Product Hunt is a curation of the best new products, every day. Discover the latest mobile apps, websites, and technology products that everyone's talking about.

STARTUPLIST
StartupList is a place to find, follow, and recommend startups. They cater to early adopters.

STARTUPTABS
The startup discovery engine. Startuptabs help you discover new startups with every tab you open.

SHOW HACKER NEWS
Show Hacker News is a way to share something that you've made on Hacker News.

ERLIBIRD
ErliBird is an early adopter and beta testing community with 40,000+ real-world users.

/R/STARTUPS
/r/startups is a community for all backgrounds, levels of expertise, and business experience.

LAUNCHING NEXT
Launching Next showcases the world's most promising new startups every day.

KILLERSTARTUPS
KillerStartups is a user driven internet startups community.

IDEASQUARES
IdeaSquares is a virtual, global space for business ideas.

PRESENTATIONS

SLIDEBEAN
Dozens of pitch deck templates for startups. Just add your content, Slidebean designs it for you.

SWIPE
With Swipe, anything can be a slide and you can present it live to anyone, anywhere, on any device.

FLOWVELLA
FlowVella is the perfect presentation software for the modern world. Create stunning presentations from your Mac or iPad – share them with anyone.

SILK
With Silk, you can publish your data online, beautifully.

SLIDESHARE
SlideShare is a LinkedIn company and the world's largest community for sharing presentations.

CHARTBLOCKS
Chartblocks is the world's easiest chart builder app. Design and share a chart in minutes.

SLIDES CARNIVAL
Slides Carnival provides you with free templates for your Google slides presentations.

PREZI
Resonate, motivate, and be remembered with Prezi, presentation software reimagined.

INFOGR.AM
Infogr.am is the world's most popular infographics creator.

HAIKU DECK
Create inspiring presentations and set your story free with Haiku Deck, available for iPad and iPhone, or on the web.

PRODUCT DEMO

DUNNNK
Upload your designs and download a final mockup within seconds.

VIDEOSCRIBE
VideoScribe is pure magic. Create your own whiteboard-style animations with no design or technical know-how.

EXPLAINIFY
Remarkable videos for business. Explainify are experts in animated video production.

PLACEIT
Make Beautiful Product Mockups & Videos with Placeit.

VIDEOBLOCKS
VideoBlocks provides unlimited download access to over 100,000 clips of stock videos, backgrounds, AE templates and more!

VIDEOLEAN
Create your product video in minutes, with Videolean.

DISSOLVE
Dissolve provides royalty-free HD footage for your product demo.

STARTUP VIDEOS
Startup Videos showcases the best explainer videos you can find on the web.

LAUNCHING

STARTUPLISTER
Startuplister helps you generate traffic and exposure by manually submitting your startup to directories, review sites, & industry blogs.

PRESSROOM.IO
Pressroom.io is the most stylish and effective way to create and update a press page for your website.

PR.CO
pr.co is the PR toolkit you will actually love and use.

PITCHPIGEON
Pitchpigeon is a pitch delivery platform for tech companies.

TINY PITCH
Create and share great looking announcements from any device using just your email with Tiny Pitch.

JUSTREACHOUT
JustReachOut is the easiest way for startups and individuals to find and pitch relevant reporters based on the best fit for topic.

LUKEWARM
Lukewarm helps you build a list of contacts from Twitter, reach out via cold emails, and then track responses.

PRESSFARM
Get a link to a journalist's email, bio and twitter with pressfarm.

NOUNCY
Use Nouncy and create a landing page, build up support and launch it with a splash of social media posts.

PUBLICIZE
Publicize wants to offer cost-effective PR solutions to entrepreneurs.

CUSTOMER SUPPORT

KATANA
Katana turns your visitors into customers with real-time video directly on your site.

ZENDESK
Zendesk is a leading cloud-based customer service software solution.

SQUARESEND
Squaresend turns your mailto links into delightful feedback forms.

FRESHDESK
Freshdesk is a cloud-based customer support software.

CASENGO

Casengo offers super simple customer service software for email, live chat, and social media.

FRONT

Front takes out the pain of shared inboxes (contact@, team@, jobs@...) by introducing collaboration in email.

USERVOICE

UserVoice integrates easy-to-use feedback, helpdesk, and knowledge base management tools in one platform.

KEEPING

Keeping is a Gmail extension that adds helpdesk functionalities to any Gmail account.

CLICKDESK

Engage your website visitors with ClickDesk - a reliable combo of Live Chat, Helpdesk, Voice and Video tools for your website.

RETAIN.CC

Send behavior-driven emails and in-app messages to your users, based on who they are and what they do, with Retain.cc.

ANALYTICS

CRAZY EGG

Through Crazy Egg's heat map and scroll map reports you can get an understanding of how your visitors engage with your website.

GECKOBOARD

Geckoboard is a real-time dashboard that gives you instant access to your most important metrics.

KISSMETRICS

KISSmetrics gives you the insights you need to optimize your marketing.

OPTIMIZELY

Optimizely is a website optimization platform that makes A/B and multivariate testing incredibly easy and powerful.

MIXPANEL

Mixpanel is the most advanced analytics platform in the world for mobile & web.

CHARTIO

Chartio is an award-winning interface to data.

SEGMENT

Segment is a single hub for customer data. Collect your customer data in one place, send it anywhere.

RESOURCES

UXCAM
Capture and visualize user behavior data to improve the usability of your app with UXCam.

TREPSCORE
TrepScore is An Intelligent Data Management System Designed For Entrepreneurs.

GOOGLE ANALYTICS
Google Analytics is a web analytics solution that gives you rich insights into your website's data.

MOBILE (APP) ANALYTICS

DISTIMO
The #1 App Analytics and the most accurate App Data. Distimo is trusted by developers worldwide to track over 345,000 apps.

FLURRY
Flurry helps 190k+ companies across 600k apps optimize the mobile experience for people everywhere.

LOCALYTICS
Localytics is a closed-loop app analytics and marketing platform that helps brands acquire, engage, and retain users.

APP ANNIE
App Annie is the leading provider of app store analytics, app rankings, and market intelligence.

COUNTLY
Countly is a self-hosted/cloud mobile application analytics & push notifications platform, developed by data scientists.

TAPLYTICS
Mobile A/B testing without App Store updates on iOS and Android. Run real time experiments and increase app revenue with Taplytics.

HEATMAPS
Heatmaps is a lightweight iOS framework that tracks individual parts of user apps to collect taps, gestures, and device interactions.

VESSEL
Make informed decisions with mobile AB testing, run A/B tests, analyze results and increase revenue with Vessel.

SEARCHMAN
App Store Optimization & SEO Software, Made Easy with SearchMan.

VUE
Make your entire team mobile analytics experts with VUE.

PROJECT MANAGEMENT

ASANA
Asana puts conversations & tasks together, so you can get more done with less effort.

BASECAMP
Basecamp is the leading web-based project management and collaboration tool. To-dos, files, messages, schedules, and milestones.

GOPLAN
Goplan is an project management and collaboration tool for individuals and teams. Tasks, Tickets, Calendar, Time tracking and Documents.

PIVOTAL TRACKER
Pivotal Tracker is an awesome, lightweight, agile project management tool for software teams.

BLOSSOM
Blossom is a very lightweight project management tool that assists people in creating the products they love.

SPRINTLY
Sprintly is an agile tool that powers a more productive relationship between development teams and their management.

WRIKE
Wrike is an advanced project management & collaboration tools for Enterprise and SMB.

TEAMGANTT
TeamGantt offers the easiest way to plan, track, and communicate on your projects.

CODEBASE
Codebase is a software project management tool with Git, Mercurial and subversion hosting.

COLLABORATION
& COMMUNICATION

TALKO
Talko is the best way to use your voice to get things done.

YAMMER
Yammer is a private social network that helps employees collaborate across departments, locations and business apps.

SLACK
Slack brings all your communication together in one place. It's real-time messaging, archiving and search for modern teams.

RESOURCES

PODIO
Podio is the online work platform. Manage, share, and get your work done smarter together with tools that work like you.

FLOWDOCK
Flowdock is a team collaboration app for desktop, mobile & web.

QUIP
Quip is a beautiful mobile productivity suite that enables you to collaborate on any device.

HIPCHAT
HipChat is group instant messaging built exclusively for teams.

REALTIMEBOARD
RealtimeBoard is your regular whiteboard, re-thought for the best online experience.

JOIN.ME
join.me provides instant screen sharing tool for ad-hoc collaborations, trainings and online meetings.

SQWIGGLE
Sqwiggle is a tool for instant tap on the shoulder remote discussions.

PRODUCTIVITY

DO
Do helps you run productive meetings. Do work you love.

FOUNDERSUITE
Foundersuite provides you with tools to get startup sh*t done.

EVERNOTE
Evernote designs apps and products that transform the way you work.

ASSISTANT.TO
Assistant.to allows you to schedule in seconds all within email. No more back and forth. No double bookings. Get it now for Gmail.

FOCUS
Focus is a Mac app that blocks distracting websites so you can boost your productivity.

SLIMWIKI
Wikis don't have to be ugly, complex and hard to manage. Welcome to the future of the Wiki, with SlimWiki.

MEETINGHERO
MeetingHero makes it easy for you and your team to have highly productive, engaging meetings.

FOREST
Forest is an app helping you stay away from your smartphone and stay focused on your work.

1PASSWORD
1Password is a password manager and secure wallet for Mac, Windows, iOS, and Android.

TIMEFUL
Timeful gets things scheduled so you can get them done. Get intelligent assistance and make the most of your time.

FEEDBACK & BUGTRACKING

DOORBELL
Easily gather in-app user feedback, on websites, iOS apps, and Android apps with Doorbell.

USERSNAP
Usersnap is a visual bug tracker for everyone working on a web project.

BUGHERD
BugHerd is the easiest way to collect client feedback, resolve issues and manage your projects.

LIGHTHOUSE
Lighthouse will help you keep track of your project development with ease.

TAPERECORDER
TapeRecorder is an SDK that allows you to record what users are doing in your app.

JIRA
Track and manage everything with JIRA project and issue tracking software by Atlassian

PROMOTER.IO
Easily measure your Net Promoter Score with Promoter.io

CRITTERCISM
Run faster, better and smarter apps with Crittercism's mobile application performance management.

ROLLBAR
Rollbar collects and analyzes errors on web and mobile apps so you can find and fix them faster.

BUGCLIPPER
Report issues directly from your app, with screenshots, screen recordings and crash videos with BugClipper.

SHOP

TICTAIL
Tictail is an ecommerce website for everyone.

RESOURCES

SHOPIFY
Build your online store with Shopify's ecommerce software and easily sell in person with Shopify's iPad POS.

SEOSHOP
SEOshop is a hosted ecommerce solution that allows you to set up and run your own online store.

NEAR ME
Near Me is a peer-to-peer commerce solution enabling anyone to setup their own branded marketplace.

BIG CARTEL
Big Cartel is a simple shopping cart for clothing and tee designers, bands, record labels, jewelry makers, crafters, and other artists.

SQUARESPACE
Squarespace lets you easily create a fully integrated ecommerce website and accept payments instantly.

LEMONSTAND
Grow beyond the limits of shopping carts built for part-time merchants with LemonStand's eCommerce platform.

SPACES
Create landing pages integrated with payments in no time, with Spaces, for free.

GUMROAD
Gumroad enables creators to sell directly to their audience — so that they can make a living doing what they love.

HIGHWIRE
Highwire Commerce allows you to create your own online store in just minutes!

PAYMENTS

CHARGEBEE
ChargeBee is an affordable subscription billing & recurring billing solution for online web apps.

RECURLY
Recurly offers enterprise-class subscription billing for thousands of companies worldwide.

ZUORA
Zuora's cloud technologies helps companies build subscription business models by establishing recurring customer relationships.

STRIPE
Stripe is a developer-friendly way to accept payments online and in mobile apps.

RESOURCES

CHARGIFY
Chargify simplifies recurring billing for Web 2.0 and SaaS companies.

PAYMILL
Paymill is the fastest and easiest way to accept payments online.

PLASSO
Plasso makes accepting and making payments quick & easy.

WEPAY
WePay is designed for platforms like marketplaces, crowdfunding sites & small business tools.

BRAINTREE
Braintree is the easiest way to accept payments online and on a mobile app. Apply online, instant approvals.

COINBASE
Coinbase is the simplest way to buy, use, and accept Bitcoin.

OUTSOURCING

ODESK
Find freelancers and freelance jobs on oDesk.

99DESIGNS
99designs is the world's largest online marketplace for design.

TOPTAL
Toptal is a marketplace where start-ups connect with top software developers.

FOLYO
Folyo helps startups find great designers by connecting them with a curated list of talented freelancers.

GIGSTER
Hire a quality developer for your project in under 5 minutes with Gigster.

FIVERR
Fiverr is the marketplace for creative & professional services.

ZIRTUAL
Zirtual is a virtual executive assistant service that matches busy people with dedicated personal assistants.

CREATIVE MARKET
Creative Market is a platform for handcrafted, mousemade design content from independent creatives around the world.

CLARITY
Clarity is your lifeline that instantly connects you with battle-tested advice from entrepreneurs.

RESOURCES

ELANCE
Find rated web developers, mobile programmers, designers, writers, translators, marketing pros, virtual assistants and more with Elance.

RAISING CAPITAL

ANGELLIST
AngelList is where the world meets startups.

DEALROOM
Dealroom gives you direct and secure access to the world's most sophisticated investors at your fingertips.

GUST
Gust connects startups with the largest collection of investors across the world.

SEEDINVEST
SeedInvest is a leading equity crowdfunding platform. They help startups raise capital online in a simple, streamlined way.

THEFUNDED
TheFunded is a guide to help entrepreneurs find the perfect funding source for their business.

F6S
f6s is where startups grow together.

ASK THE VC
Standard forms of documents used for early stage financings, provided by Ask The VC.

CAPTABLE.IO
Captable.io is a simple tool for recording and sharing your startup's captable.

SHAREWAVE
Sharewave is the best way to manage shareholders.

FOUNDRS
Calculate Founders Equity with the Foundrs calculator.

INVESTOR RELATIONS

UPDATE MY VC
Update My VC is a modern guide to keeping in touch with your investors.

HOCKEYSTICK
Hockeystick gets investors engaged and active.

SEEDERBOARD
Seederboard is a communications platform which helps companies in funding stages between seed and IPO.

SHARKBOARD
Sharkboard connects unlisted companies with their stakeholders.

CODING VC
A template for your update emails to your investors.

XTENSIO
Show your company's strengths, latest information and progress with Xtensio.

VISIBLE
Visible takes the pain out of reporting.

OPSTARTS
Opstarts makes planning and forecasting simple.

REPORTALLY
Reportally offers investor reporting and board governance for startups and SMEs.

GROW
Grow is the simplest BI dashboard software available.

SALES

LEADGENIUS
LeadGenius provides delightfully simple sales and marketing services for your growing business.

CLOSE.IO
Close.io is the inside sales CRM of choice for SMBs.

RECEIPTFUL
Start increasing your Customer Lifetime Value for free today with Receiptful.

FILEBOARD
Present, ScreenShare and Track Results from your Slide Decks and Live Sales Calls with Fileboard.

MATTERMARK
Mattermark provides the leading research tools for understanding the world of private companies.

VOILANORBERT
VoilaNorbert aims to help people find anyone email address by only having their full name and company domain.

SIDEKICK
Sidekick is a free service that gives you email superpowers with contact insights, email tracking, and email scheduling.

SELL HACK
Use Sell Hack To Extend Social Profiles with a HACK IN button and uncover more data.

SPARTA
Sparta helps sales teams drive revenue growth and reach their potential with a simple to use sales gamification platform.

CRM

FULLCONTACT FOR GMAIL
Know everything about your Gmail contacts, right from your inbox with Full-Contact for Gmail.

STREAK
Streak is the easiest way to manage business processes in Gmail.

PARDOT
Pardot provides no-hassle marketing automation.

HIGHRISE
Highrise is your secret weapon to track tasks, contacts, and notes.

INTERCOM
More than 4,000 web and mobile businesses use Intercom to connect with customers. They have live conversations inside their products and send targeted email and in-app messages, triggered by time or behavior.

REFRESH
Discover common ground for better conversations with Refresh.

VTIGER
Vtiger helps small and mid-sized businesses become more customer centric.

RELATEIQ
RelateIQ is rethinking customer relationship management to help you drive more revenue.

CONTACTUALLY
Contactually automatically reminds you to stay connected with your top leads.

CHARLIE
Charlie automatically briefs you on people before you see them.

LEGAL

TERMSFEED
Generate Privacy Policy, Terms and Conditions with TermsFeed.

CONTRACTUALLY
Use Contractually to keep momentum in your business by collaborating online with your business partners and customers.

ROCKET LAWYER
Manage all of your legal needs online with Rocket Lawyer.

SNAPTERMS
Snapterms is a simple, fast and effective solution for terms of service, privacy policies and more for your website.

DOCRACY
Docracy is the web's only open collection of legal contracts and the best way to negotiate and sign documents online.

LEGALZOOM
LegalZoom is the nation's leading provider of personalized, online legal solutions and legal documents for small business owners and families.

STARTUP DOCUMENTS
Startup Documents streamlines the incorporation and legal document process for founders and lawyers.

UPCOUNSEL
Get high-quality legal services from top business attorneys at reasonable rates with UpCounsel.

DOCSTOC
Docstoc provides the best quality & widest selection of documents and resources to start and grow your small business.

DOCUSIGN
Securely sign and manage documents online from any device with DocuSign.

FINANCE

SUSH.IO
Sush.io, All your SaaS and Online apps. Get Business Analytics with smart automations!

FREE INVOICE GENERATOR
Easy to use free invoice template to create invoices in PDF.

FRESHBOOKS
FreshBooks is the #1 cloud accounting solution.

BALLPARK
Thousands of small businesses use Ballpark to send invoices, receive payments, bid on projects, and keep their team on the same page.

FREEAGENT
FreeAgent is accounting software for small businesses and freelancers.

EXPENSIFY
Expensify is the best expense reporting app on your phone & web.

STARTUP FINANCIAL MODEL
The Startup Financial Model walks you through the important questions of creating a credible financial plan step-by-step.

ZENPAYROLL
ZenPayroll is the most delightful — and only — payroll service you'll ever use.

CHARGEDESK
Use ChargeDesk and integrate Stripe, Braintree, WePay & PayPal with Zendesk.

HR

RECRUITEE
Recruitee is a collaborative hiring platform. It combines four products in one: employer branding, job promoting, talent sourcing, and applicant tracking.

HOMERUN
Homerun enables your company to create authentic job openings, receive richer applications and review applicants faster and more effective.

KIN
Kin HR Software streamlines HR for your entire team.

PLAYBOOK HR
Playbook HR offers an applicant tracking system for independent workforces.

NAMELY
Namely is the leading end-to-end HR, payroll, and benefits platform for growing companies.

WORKABLE
Workable is a beautifully simple tool to advertise jobs and make better hiring decisions with your team.

LESSON.LY
Lesson.ly is the easy training software.

LEVER
Lever is a modern web app for organizing your hiring.

THE RESUMATOR
The Resumator's applicant tracking system & resume database will help you make great hires every time.

TYBA
Tyba matches fast-growing companies with the talent that'll drive them forward.

LEARNING

STARTUP PODCAST
StartUp is a podcast series about what happens when someone who knows nothing about business starts one.

STARTUPSANONYMOUS
StartupsAnonymous is a place for startups to share stories and ask questions anonymously.

DORM ROOM TYCOON
Dorm Room Tycoon is the podcast show that interviews the world's most influential innovators.

UDACITY
Udacity online courses bridge the gap between real world skills, relevant education, and employment.

HOW TO START A STARTUP
Everything we know about how to start a startup, for free, from some of the world experts.

MIXERGY
Mixergy is where entrepreneurs & authors — Seth Godin, Guy Kawasaki, Paul Graham, Eric Ries, Barbara Corcoran & more — teach ambitious upstarts.

GOOGLE VENTURES LIBRARY
Get advice on everything from product management to workspace design, inside the Google Ventures Library.

STARTUP{ERY
Startup{ery gathers and organizes the best resources to help you build your business.

ROCKETSHIP.FM
Learn about product development, funding, bootstrapping, sales, and growth via Rocketship.fm.

VIDEOS

THIS WEEK IN STARTUPS
Tech entrepreneur Jason Calacanis hosts discussion of the startup news that matters.

FOUNDATION
Foundation is a monthly video series interviewing influential founders in the tech community.

STARTUPTALKS
StartupTalks is procrastination for professionals.

50 GROUNDBREAKING STARTUP IDEAS
50 startup founders discussing the origins of their ideas.

GROWTH HACKER TV
Trying to grow a startup? Hustlers don't watch cable, they watch Growth Hacker TV. New episodes released weekly.

SANDWICH VIDEO
Sandwich Video makes videos, mostly for neat tech products.

#STARTUPMOVIES
#StartupMovies offers the best movies, series and geeks documentaries featuring startups and entrepreneurs.

SMALL EMPIRES
Small Empires is The Verge's weekly show on rising startups.

THE #ASKGARYVEE SHOW
You ask questions, Gary Vaynerchuck will try to answer them.

STARTUP GRIND VIDEOS
Startup Grind is a global startup community designed to educate, inspire, and connect entrepreneurs.

BLOGS

THE HOW
A new approach to startup management from field-tested entrepreneurs.

FELD THOUGHTS
Brad Feld is a VC at Foundry Group and invests in software and Internet companies around the US.

VENTUREBEAT
VentureBeat is the leading source for news & perspective on tech innovation.

VENTURE HACKS
Startup advice from the founders of AngelList (@nivi and @naval).

FIRST ROUND BLOG
First Round is a seed-stage venture firm focused on building a vibrant community of technology entrepreneurs and companies.

BEN'S BLOG
Ben Horowitz is a VC at Andreessen Horowitz and the author of the book "The hard thing about hard things".

BOTH SIDES OF THE TABLE
Mark Suster is a 2x entrepreneur turned VC. He is a partner at Upfront Ventures, focused on early-stage technology companies.

SAM ALTMAN'S BLOG
Sam Altman is an entrepreneur, programmer, venture capitalist and blogger. He is the president of Y Combinator.

CHRIS DIXON'S BLOG
Chris Dixon is a General Partner at Andreessen Horowitz.

SPRINGWISE
Springwise scans the globe for smart new business ideas, delivering instant inspiration to entrepreneurial minds.

NEWSLETTERS

LAUNCH DIGEST
Launch Digest brings you lessons learned from product launches.

LAUNCH TICKER
The LAUNCH Ticker is a daily newsletter that curates the top stories in tech everyday.

THE MATTERMARK DAILY
Get first-person accounts of entrepreneurship with The Mattermark Daily.

SIDEBAR
Every day, Sidebar delivers you the 5 best design links curated by a selection of great editors.

IOS DEV WEEKLY
The Best of iOS Development, Delivered Weekly, for free.

THE UX NEWSLETTER.
Stories about designing, researching and building all things MailChimp.

HACKER NEWSLETTER
The Hacker News Newsletter.

LETTERLIST
Discover Awesome Newsletters.

CHARGED
Charged is a handcrafted newsletter with the most interesting stories on tech/startups.

THE SUNDAY DISPATCHES
Weekly articles to help you be a better creative.

BUILDING/CODING TOOLS – LEARN TO CODE

Codecademy – FREE – interactive code tutorials.
Khan Academy – FREE – Tons of coding tutorials and classes.
PHPmaster – FREE – PHP tutorials and discussions.
CodeAvenger – FREE – HTML/CSS and JavaScript for beginners-intermediate.
Tizag – FREE – Simple tutorials and cheat sheets for html, css, and php.
Code School – $25/Month – Ruby/GIT/Backbone.js/JQuery/Java/HTML/iOS Objective C and much more.
Lynda – Starting at $25/month – More than 1500 online video courses in a wide variety of fields, including many coding languages.
Treehouse – Tiered plans from $25/month – $49/month – Same concept as Lynda, but strictly for coding. Crazy in-depth programs.
Skillshare – Price varies and depends on the class and teacher – In-person and online classes based around many different subjects, including many coding topics/classes.
tutsplus – starting at $19/month – Hundreds of coding video courses/tutorials.
(9/5/13) Open Education Database – A huge database/repository of Free Online Engineering & Computer Science Classes from top universities.

DEV PLATFORMS AND PROGRAMS

ToolsCloud – Tons of Dev tools.
FuseGrid – ColdFusion cloud hosting. Full disclosure- I have no idea what that means.
CodeAnywhere – Code editor in a browser with native clients on Android, iOS, and BlackBerry.
Bootstrap – Front-end framework by Twitter.
Heroku – Super-easy app deployment.
FriendCode – Free private repositories and collaboration.
Firebug – Firefox Dev platform.
CodeVisually – a repository of coding tools and resources.
Google Page Speed Test – Loading speed insights.
uTest – All things testing. UX/security/functionality/speed/localization/load testing.
Fivesecondtest – Crowdsourced landing page optimization.
Silverback – Usability testing software.

SOURCING, VERSION CONTROL, INTEGRATION AND DEPLOYMENT

dotCloud – Affordable custom application stacks.
Parse – Cloud app platform for iOS, Android, JavaScript, Windows 8, Windows Phone 8, and OS X.
Binpress – High-quality source code discovery and marketplace.
Cloud9 IDE – Run and debug Node.js and JavaScript code, and also supports running Python, Ruby, and Apache+PHP applications.
OffScale – Database version management.
Bitbucket – Private repository hosting.
Pixelapse – Design version control, backup, and collaboration.
memsql – World's fastest in memory database.
GitHub – Collaboration, review, and code management for open source and private development projects.
Hostedci – Hosted continuous integration for iOS and Mac.
Wercker – Continuous delivery SaaS.
CircleCI – Continuous Integration and Deployment.
TestPilot.me – Continuous integration.

BUG TRACKING AND USER FEEDBACK

PivotalTracker – Bug tracking and project management platform.
Crittercism – Mobile app performance management platform.
BugHerd – Bug tracking, user feedback, and project management platform.
BugSense – Mobile app bug tracking.
Rollbar – Error collection and analysis.
Usernap – Visual design and bug feedback/tracking.
Crashlytics – App crash/error analytics.
UserTesting.com – User Testing. Simple enough.
Usabilla – Visualize user feedback.
Qualaroo – User behavior dependent prompts.
Kampyle – User feedback forms.
GutCheck – On-demand user insights community.
WebEngage – Survey your users.

MISCELLANEOUS TOOLS

Notepad++ – Open-source code editor.
SeaMonkey – Open-source all in one internet app suite.
BlueGriffion – Open-source Firefox editor.
Trellian WebPage – Robust open-source dev tool kit.
Wufoo – Form builder.
FormStack – Form builder.
EdenPHP – Huge PHP library.
Firebase – Backend maintenance as a service.
Snippets.me – Code snippet manager/storage.

DESIGN TOOLS & UI/UX RESOURCES

SubtlePatterns – Pattern/texture repository.
Divshot – Interface builder for web applications.
Scratchpad – UI for dummies. Platform allows you to grab and collect UI elements from anywhere on the web.
Balsamiq – Rapid wireframe/mock-ups tool.
Mockingbird – Collaborative wireframing tool.
Lucidchart – Collaborative Wireframing/mind-mapping/diagraming tool that integrates with Google Drive.
AppCooker – Clickable iPhone and iPad app mockups.
FluidUI – Mobile prototyping for iOS, Android, and Windows.

MOBILE TOOLS (BUILDING/CODING)

Appcelerator – Mobile app development platform.
PhoneGap – Free open-source framework that utilizes APIs, HTML, CSS, and Java.
Flurry – Development/analytics/advertising/monitization platform for iOS, Android, BlackBerry, and Windows mobile apps.
AppCodes – App Store SEO platform for your app.
StackMob – App Back-end as a service.
AppHarbor – Hosted .NET platform as a service.
Kinvey – App back-end as a service.
Kickfolio – In browser iOS app testing.

DESIGN

AppCooker – Mock-ups and wire-framing with clickable prototypes.
Codiqa – Super-fast mobile prototyping. Native apps and mobile websites.
Prototypes – iOS prototyping.
UXPin – UX design tools.
Justinmind – Interactive wire-framing.
UI Stencils – UI Stencils for hand designing apps.
Mockability – An iPhone app designed for designing iPhone apps.

CHEAPER AND FREE PHOTOSHOP AND ILLUSTRATOR ALTERNATIVES

Pixlr – Free – Web-based photo/image editor. A lot of functionality, but does not save or open many PS or vector formats. Good for simple edits on a computer or device you don't normally work on.
Pinta – Open-Source – Pretty robust tools/effects. I haven't ever used Pinta, but it looks solid, and I have heard nothing but good things.
Paint.net – Open-source – This I have used. As far as a free PS alternative goes, Paint.net is as good as it gets. Huge dev. community and tons of extensions, plugins, and brushes.
Pixelmator – $14.99 – PS alternative for Mac OS X. I haven't used Pixelmator, but it looks pretty robust, and at 15 bucks it is super affordable.
Inkscape – Open-Source – Vector graphics editor. More of an alternative to Corel or Illustrator that PS. Pretty functional, and easy to use.
Gimp – Open-Source – Robust PS alternative that supports nearly every PS and vector format.
3DVIA Shapes – Free – 3D shape and image creator/editor.

GRAPHIC DESIGN – TOOLS & RESOURCES

FindIcons – Huge database of icons and icon sets.
DesignKindle – Icons/graphics/vectors and tons of resources.
ColorMunki – Color palette creator.
Kuler – Tons of color palettes and design themes.
ColourLovers – Colors, patterns, and palettes.
Design Resource Box – CSS3, HTML5, and jQuery cheat sheets.
Color Scheme Designer – Color scheme tool.
Color Picker – An experiment by Nathan Speller that crawls through Dribbble and displays the most common palettes for any given color.
Brusheezy – Free Phostoshop brushes.
Visual.ly – Infographic creating tools and marketplace.
StatWing – Data visualization tools.
Tableau Public – Data visualization and infographic creation tools.
Infogr.am – Infographic creation tools.
PiktoChart – Infographic creation tools.

INSPIRATION AND DESIGN COMMUNITIES

Designspiration – Sort-of Pinterest for designers.
David Airey – Blog of a brand-identity designer. Lots of interesting insights.
Design Milk – Design blog tracing new and interesting work across all mediums.
SmashingMagazine – Awesome design resource. Put this in your bookmarks right now!
WebDesignerDepot – Design blog.
Twistedsifter – Similar to Design Milk, but but a different presentation and focus.
Abduzeedo – Design inspiration and tutorials.
Dribbble – Show and tell for designers.
Hunie – Hunie is an invite-only design community. It is similar to Dribbble, but more constructive and more feature-rich.

STOCK AND PUBLIC-DOMAIN IMAGES AND FONT/TYPOGRAPHY RESOURCES

Wikipedia's huge list of Public Domain Image Resources
rgbstock – Completely free.
FreeRange – Free after sign-up.
EveryStockPhoto – Free after sign-up.
Pixabay
morgueFile
VectorFinder – A stock image search engine.
Most NASA images are free to use – here are the usage guidelines.
123RF – Cheap royalty free images.
Designious – Cheap vector packs, Photoshop brushes, and hand drawn illustrations.
MediaLoot – Cheap vector packs, textures, icons, and other images.
UrbanFonts – Tons of free and paid fonts and dingbats.
dafont.com – Free, public-domain, and demo fonts.
Google Fonts – Tons of open-source fonts.
FontFeed – Premium fonts and recommendations.

CRM AND ANALYTICS/METRICS TOOLS

Apslar – Analytics and advertising platform.
Placed – Location analytics for mobile.
Appboy – Customer engagement and analytics platform.
Mixpanel – Engagement analytics.
Kontagent – Customer intelligence and segmentation.
UserMetrix – Engagement and use analytics.
Tracelytics – Stack application tracing.
Metricfire – Application metrics as a service.

TURNKEY MOBILE APPLICATIONS

hull – Social apps creator – TechStars Boulder 2013.
Mobile Roadie – Robust turnkey app creator.
Appery.io – Turnkey apps for enterprise.
AppBreeder – iPhone app templates.
BiznessApps – Apps for SMBs.

INTERACTIVE LISTS

List.ly
Listnerd

SOURCING, DATA, AND RESEARCH TOOLS

HARO (Help A Reporter Out) – Source or be a source.
Pew Research Center – Tons of data sets and info.
Amazon's Public Data Sets – Easily integrated into AWS Apps and sites.
SBA.gov – U.S. Small Business Administration's data sets.
Data.gov – U.S. Govt's public data sets.
BigML blog post – Tons of links to data sets.
SourceBottle – Connecting sources with journalists.
World Bank Data Sets – International econ. data and statistics.
IMF Data Sets – International econ. data and statistics.

DISCOVERY

YourVersion – Content discover/bookmarking around topics.
Trapit – iOS app that learns and adapts is discovery process to your tastes.
digg
Alternion – Aggregation/discovery tool.
StumbleUpon – Pure content discovery. Pick some topics and start stumbling.
The platform adapts to your thumb-ups and downs to bring you the content
that you want.

HIRING AND OUTSOURCING

SimplyHired, Indeed, Monster, Craigslist, LinkedIn – The usual job-listing
suspects.
Dice.com, TechJobs.com, – Job boards exclusivity for tech sector jobs.
AngelList Jobs – Angel.co's talent portal.
Inside Startups – Pretty cool website that allows you to take a deeper look at
startups, and post and apply for jobs.
Social Check – A tool that gives you deeper insights into applicants and po-
tential employees.
InternMatch – Find a great intern.
GroupTalent – Find a great developer or designer.
Recruiterbox – Recruitment software.
InterviewStreet – Interactive test/challenge to find the right coder.
37Signals Job Board – List or apply to many programming jobs.
Guru, Freelancer, Elance, oDesk – General tech-focused freelance databases.
99designs, CrowdSpring, DesignCrowd – Graphic design specific freelance
databases.

Made in the USA
Middletown, DE
12 March 2020

86060279R00057